Singapore

Singapore

BY WIL MARA

Enchantment of the World™
Second Series

CHILDREN'S PRESS®

An Imprint of Scholastic Inc.

Frontispiece: **Marina Bay Sands resort**

Consultant: Stephen Dobbs, Associate Professor, Asian Studies, University of Western Australia, Crawley, Australia

Please note: All statistics are as up-to-date as possible at the time of publication.

Book production by The Design Lab

Library of Congress Cataloging-in-Publication Data
Mara, Wil, author.
 Singapore / by Wil Mara.
   pages cm. — (Enchantment of the world)
 Includes bibliographical references and index.
 ISBN 978-0-531-23297-2 (library binding : alk. paper)
 1. Singapore—Juvenile literature. I. Title.
 DS609.M37 2016
 959.57—dc23   2015028181

1 2 3 4 5 6 7 8 9 10 R 25 24 23 22 21 20 19 18 17 16

Performer, Chinese New Year parade

Contents

Left to right: **Coastline, crimson sunbird, Buddhist praying, Stefanie Sun, girls**

CHAPTER 1

Growing Up

SIXTEEN-YEAR-OLD AMAYA IS LYING IN BED ON a calm, clear night, looking at the full moon through her window. Her room is on the second floor of a big and beautiful home where she lives with her older brother, Nengyi, and her parents. Her father has a good job in a chemical plant, and her mother works as a teacher of three different languages: English, Malay, and Tamil. Amaya herself speaks, writes, and reads all three fluently. Like most of her friends, she was brought up in a multilingual household. Her brother and father also speak other languages. In her country, it is common for people to know more than one.

Amaya lives in Singapore, a small, wealthy nation in Southeast Asia. Singapore is located just at the end of the Malay Peninsula, separated from the nation of Malaysia by a

Opposite: **A mother and daughter in Singapore. As of 2015, Singaporean women were having fewer children than women in any other country in the world. Women in Singapore have an average of 0.81 children.**

In Singapore, skyscrapers tower over nearby nineteenth-century shops.

narrow strait. As a result, many people of Malay background live in the country. Large numbers of Indians also live in Singapore, but most Singaporeans trace their heritage back to China.

Working Hard

Amaya is tired tonight, just like she is most every night. She had a very long day today—getting up early, going to school, and then coming home and doing a lot of homework. After that, she ate dinner and helped clean up. She and her family

Singapore is extremely ethnically diverse, and it does not have one single system for people's names.

The majority of the population is of Chinese descent. The Chinese practice is to put the family name first, followed by the given names. Take, for example, Lee Kuan Yew, Singapore's former prime minister. His "first names" were Kuan Yew, and his family name was Lee, so he would be called Mr. Lee.

Singaporeans of Malay descent typically follow Muslim practices. They do not have Western-style family names. Instead, a boy has a given name followed by the word *bin*, which means "son of," followed by his father's name. A girl has a given name followed by the word *bint* (daughter of), followed by her father's name.

Indians are the third major ethnic group in Singapore. Many Indians did not traditionally have family names, but they are becoming more common now.

then watched a little TV, but by nine o'clock she was exhausted.

Amaya gets excellent grades in school, and she knows that's because she works hard at her studies. There are times when she

Teenagers in Singapore spend an average of nine and a half hours a week on homework.

doesn't feel like doing her schoolwork, but she pushes herself to do it anyway. She has a fear inside that makes her want to do well. For as long as she can remember, the expectations for her to succeed have been very high. She knows her parents love her, but she gets the feeling they'd be deeply disappointed if she came home one day with a bad grade on her report card.

In addition, the government in her country always seems

A teacher leads a class at an Islamic school in Singapore. Islamic schools teach both traditional school subjects and religion.

to be coming up with some new program or public slogan designed to inspire her to try harder and do better. Every minute of the day, it seems, there is some kind of invisible force nudging her and her friends to achieve. She feels that pressure constantly. She's not against the idea of being successful, but sometimes she gets so worried by it that she almost feels sick to her stomach. That's why she can't sleep tonight—she has a big math test in the morning and wants to get a perfect grade.

Looking Toward the Future

Amaya is not sure what she wants to do when she grows up. She's fairly certain she doesn't want to work at the chemical plant like her father. Nor does she want to be a teacher like her

A Singaporean teenager sells cakes at a market stall. In Singapore, teens between the ages of thirteen and sixteen may work a few hours a day, but not in factories or at other dangerous sites.

mother. She has a natural artistic talent and likes to draw and paint. But she can't help noticing there aren't a lot of jobs available for people with those skills. She's getting to the age where she will soon have to decide what kind of career path to take. She's concerned, though, that she'll choose something to please her parents rather than something that really interests her.

She doesn't know too much about economics, but she is aware that just about everyone in her country who wants a job has one—and she knows that's a good thing. She would like to make good money and have a nice home. She'd like to have a family. She doesn't really worry about whether or not this is possible—she just worries whether or not she'll be happy. Everything seems almost preplanned in her life—go to school, get a car, get a job, get married, have children, work for years and years, then retire. It's all so *predictable*. Where are the surprises?

She turns over, away from the window and the full moon. *There's no time for such thoughts right now*, she tells herself. *You have that test tomorrow, and that's all that matters*. She closes her eyes and finally falls asleep.

A student dozes off while reading on the train. According to some surveys, more than half of high school students in Singapore get just six hours of sleep a night.

CHAPTER 2

Island Nation

SINGAPORE IS AN ISLAND GROUP IN SOUTHEAST Asia. The main island, Singapore Island, is shaped roughly like a long diamond. It sits at the southern tip of the Malaysian Peninsula—the nation of Malaysia is its closest neighbor—with some islands of Indonesia not far off its southwestern and southeastern coasts. The narrow Johor Strait runs to the north of Singapore Island, separating Singapore from Malaysia. The Singapore Strait lies to the south, and beyond it are islands in Indonesia. Singapore Strait is one of the busiest straits in all of Asia because it provides a deep waterway where large ships can travel.

Opposite: **A misty morning along the Singapore coast**

Many Islands

Singapore includes more than sixty other islands. These are all much smaller than the main island, and most are off the southern coast. Some of these islands are artificial. For

Singapore's Geographic Features

Area: 278 square miles (720 sq km)

Northernmost Point: Coast of Sembawang, around the Senoko Industrial Estate

Southernmost Point: Satumu Island

Westernmost Point: Tuas Island

Easternmost Point: Pedra Branca Island

Highest Elevation: Timah Hill, 531 feet (162 m) above sea level

Lowest Elevation: Sea level along the coasts

Hottest Month: June, with an average temperature of about 82°F (28°C)

Coolest Month: January, with an average temperature of about 79°F (26°C)

Most Rainy Days: November and December, with an average of 19 rainy days

Fewest Rainy Days: February, with an average of about 11 rainy days

Average Annual Precipitation: 92 inches (234 cm)

Lights brighten Jurong Island, the site of many chemical plants.

example, Jurong Island, which sits to the southwest, was created through landfill to provide a large industrial area, since virtually all potential industrial sites on Singapore Island were occupied. Today, it is home to sites that make plastics and automotive parts and process oil and gas. Other large islands include Tekong, Ubin, and Sentosa.

Although Singapore is very small, it has a major economic impact throughout Asia and beyond, because it is a wealthy country. Singapore Island is just over 31 miles (50 kilometers) from east to west and about 16 miles (26 km) from north to south. In total, the country has a land area of merely 278 square miles (720 sq km), making it just a quarter of the size of the U.S. state of Rhode Island!

Timah Hill rises to an elevation of more than 500 feet (150 m), but most of Singapore lies less than 50 feet (15 m) above sea level.

Lay of the Land

The land in Singapore is relatively flat. The majority of it lies just barely above sea level. The center of the main island features rugged hills. The tallest, Timah Hill, reaches 531 feet (162 meters) above sea level. Other hills in this region include Panjang and Mandai. A plateau stretches across the eastern section of Singapore Island. Low valleys mark the flat land.

Many streams cut across the land in Singapore. During severe storms, these streams cannot take up all the rain that falls, and flooding is common.

Hot and Wet

Singapore sits near the equator, the imaginary line that circles Earth halfway between the North and South Poles. Lands near the equator are in the tropical zone. They are typically characterized by high temperatures and humidity, as well as lots of rainfall. In Singapore, the temperatures are pretty much the same throughout the year. The average high temperature for the entire year is 88 degrees Fahrenheit (31 degrees Celsius). Nighttime temperatures drop 10 to 15°F (6 to 8°C) at the most.

Singapore's many warm days are ideal for a visit to the beach or a bicycle ride.

Singapore is also extremely humid. The water hangs in the atmosphere, making it seem even hotter than it is. The western half of the island experiences much more rainfall than the eastern side, and thus is a bit cooler while remaining more humid.

Singapore experiences two distinct rainy seasons, also known as monsoon seasons. A monsoon is a seasonal wind that typically blows in from the ocean, often bringing heavy

rain. Singapore's Northeast Monsoon season runs from mid-autumn to early spring. During this time of the year, the winds come from the northeast. During the Southeast Monsoon season, which runs from early summer to early fall, winds come from the southeast. Monsoon seasons sometimes bring rain and winds for days at a time. Over the course of the year, Singapore receives nearly 100 inches (250 centimeters) of rainfall, with anywhere from ten to twenty rainy days during a given month, depending on the season.

Growing City

A few decades ago, Singapore had a busy city center along the southern coast of Singapore Island, near the busy shipping ports. The rest of the country was a mix of forest, farmland, and the hills and valleys of the northwest. In recent decades, however, Singapore has become more urbanized. This evolution began back in the 1960s. At the time, the city center, now known as the Central Area, was the mainstay of business activity, but there were some other industrial areas on the island. Today, the entire country is almost one giant city.

Ubin Island is one of the few undeveloped parts of Singapore. Once the site of many stone quarries where granite was cut from the ground, it is now a protected bird habitat.

The land has become so built up that the government has to plan all future developments while carefully managing what's already there. The government ensures that the land is used sensibly, that pollution is minimized, and that transportation is efficient. In industrial parks, many businesses, even if they are large, often share the same land. Almost all new industries on the main island produce little or no air pollution. Businesses that create more pollution are generally relegated to industrialized island areas, such as Jurong Island.

Although a significant part of Singapore's main island is urban, the government does try to maintain a natural presence. To that end, about half of the island's land is occupied by trees or other plants. Singapore also has a few nature reserves as well as more than three hundred parks and recreation areas.

Natural Resources

Singapore has few natural resources, in part because the land is so developed. Only about 5 percent of the land is forested.

This lack of resources can create major problems. Getting enough clean water, for example, is a continual challenge for the nation. Singapore has virtually no sources of fresh water, such as lakes or rivers. Thus, in the past, most of the fresh water the people of Singapore could use came from rainfall. In dry times, water had to be imported from neighboring nations. More recently, the government has attempted to address the issue in a variety of ways. Singapore has started to build desalination plants, where salt can be removed from ocean water

Government officials toured Singapore's first desalination plant during its official opening in 2005.

to make the water usable for drinking and irrigation. Another approach is called reverse osmosis. This system reuses wastewater, which includes everything from the water that goes down the drain in the bathroom or kitchen to the rainwater that runs across a street and down through a grate. This water is treated until it is clean and usable again. Reverse osmosis has been highly successful. Still, the problem of acquiring enough water is far from solved.

Boys play in a fountain in the Singapore Botanic Gardens. Singapore gets fresh water from a variety of sources.

Singapore also has limited sources of energy. It has no reserves of coal, oil, or natural gas. Because of this, it has to import them from other nations. In 2001, the government made the decision to convert most of the electrical plants to run on natural gas. Today, natural gas is used to produce about 80 percent of Singapore's electricity.

Singapore has not taken advantage of sunlight and wind as renewable sources of energy. The government has been slow to respond to these options and has not encouraged the installation of solar panels and wind turbines. However, the government has been trying to make use of a different renewable energy source—biomass. This is biological matter such as leaves, wood, and animal bones, which can be used to produce energy as they decay.

An oil refinery on the coast of Singapore, one of Asia's leading oil-refining nations

CHAPTER 3

Wild and Free

OVER THE LAST TWO CENTURIES, AS SINGAPORE has industrialized and grown in population, the rich variety of life-forms that once lived there has diminished. Two centuries ago, the island of Singapore hosted a lush rain forest environment teeming with plants and animals. But in 1819, the British established a trading post on the island. The trading post attracted people and businesses to Singapore, which thrived in the following decades. This led to Singapore's industrialization and population growth, which ultimately had a devastating effect on the island's plants and animals. Experts estimate that about 95 percent of the forest that once covered the land is gone. Roughly a third of Singapore's native species have become extinct. About half of all the surviving species on the island live only in areas protected by the government. These reserves constitute just a tiny portion of available land.

Opposite: **The brightly colored crimson sunbird grows only about 4 inches (10 cm) long. Many people consider it the national bird of Singapore.**

Singapore Zoo

Although Singapore does not have much wild space, the nation does have several zoos and preserves where visitors can see extraordinary creatures. The Singapore Zoo, which opened in 1973, now features more than three hundred species that live in environments that resemble their natural habitats as closely as possible. Highlights include the largest captive population of orangutans in the world and three rare white tigers, which have white fur, brown stripes, and blue eyes. The zoo draws more than 1.5 million visitors each year and now includes animal research and rescue as part of its operations.

Plant Life

About 1,400 plant species grow in Singapore, but about half of them are now considered endangered. Plants grow wild and free in only a few areas, so Singaporeans tend to be familiar mainly with nonnative plants that are found in city areas and are maintained for decoration. The nation has hundreds of parks and four nature reserves. Efforts are being made to establish new forests. Most of these efforts are privately funded and run by volunteers, but the Singaporean government does support them.

Mangroves and More

Some of the most frequently seen trees in Singapore are mangroves. Mangroves are unusual in that they can grow in salt water, their long roots emerging from beneath the water. Mangrove forests are important because they protect the coastline from strong waves and erosion and because their tangle of roots serves as a safe habitat for small fish and other sea creatures. Sungei Buloh Wetland Reserve on Singapore's northern coast includes a mangrove boardwalk where visitors can get a close view of this rich habitat.

Other notable plant species in Singapore include the tembusu tree. It is found throughout Southeast Asia and is characterized by a very dark bark that has deep grooves running throughout. It produces light green leaves and yellowish flowers. The tembusu tree is known for having remarkably sturdy, long-lasting wood that resists infestation by termites and similar insects. The tree itself is resilient and can thrive in a variety of environments. The

The roots of mangrove trees rise like fingers out of the shallow salt water at Sungei Buloh Wetland Reserve.

Singaporeans are so proud of the tembusu that it is featured on the back of their five-dollar bills.

Also interesting is the Singapore cherry tree. This tough tree grows quickly and is able to thrive in harsh conditions. For example, it can survive in places where it gets very little water; places where other trees cannot. The Singapore cherry tree seldom reaches a height of more than about 36 feet (11 m) and produces a sweet fruit that is cherished by animals and people. The fruit is often used to make drinks or spreads, and it is sometimes used for medicinal purposes. Despite its name, the Singapore cherry

Tembusu trees sometimes grow 130 feet (40 m) tall. For much of the year, tembusus are covered with white flowers that give off a strong scent at dawn and sunset.

is not native to Singapore. Its normal range isn't even on that side of the world. Rather, it is native to parts of the Western Hemisphere, including Mexico, Central America, and north-western South America. No one is certain how the species found its way to Asia, but it is well established there, growing not just in Singapore but in many neighbor nations as well, including India.

One of Singapore's rarest species is the Singapore bonsai. This small tree grows along the border of mangrove forests or among the rocky edges of ocean shorelines. Its tough, dense wood helps it thrive in such harsh environments. These qualities also make it ideal for carving and building, but the tree is so rare that cutting it down is prohibited by law. The Singapore bonsai also grows in other Asian nations as well as in parts of Africa and Australia. It is not, however, common in any of these locales.

The fruit of the Singapore cherry is sweet and is often used to make jams and tea.

Meet Vanda Miss Joaquim

The national flower of Singapore is the Singapore orchid, which is also known as Vanda Miss Joaquim. Unlike most national flowers, the Singapore orchid is not naturally occurring. Instead, it is a hybrid, a cross between a Burmese orchid and a Malayan orchid. It was created in the late 1800s by a Singaporean woman named Agnes Joaquim who was an expert in horticulture—the science of growing plants. The beautiful orchid—primarily a rich medium pink with highlights both lighter and darker—was named the national flower of Singapore in 1981. It was chosen in part because it is hardy and blooms year-round. Because it is a hybrid, it is considered to represent Singapore's mix of cultures.

Many Creatures

Despite being heavily urbanized, Singapore is home to a broad variety of animals. There are more than 350 different bird species, 150 types of reptiles and amphibians, about 50 kinds of mammals, and more than 2,000 different fish species and other creatures found in the coastal waters. Many other creatures native to Singapore have gone extinct in the last two centuries. Those that remain have managed to adapt to the way humans have radically changed the environment.

Mammals

One of the best-adapted mammals in this regard is the crab-eating macaque. It is a small, gray-brown monkey that rarely weighs more than 18 pounds (8 kilograms), about the size of a large house cat. The crab-eating macaque is a widespread species that seems to have little trouble sharing space with humans. It is frequently seen in cities, but its preferred habitat is the forest. It is an opportunistic feeder, eating whatever it can find. The largest part of its diet is usually fruit, but it also eats flowers, seeds, birds, lizards, frogs, and fish. Despite its name, crabs are not a big part of crab-eating macaques' diet. Some macaques that live near mangrove forests, however, have learned to dive underwater to catch crabs and other ocean creatures.

A young crab-eating macaque chews on a piece of plant.

A young pangolin climbs on its mother. The name *pangolin* comes from a Malay word, *pengguling,* which means "something that rolls up."

Other large mammals that live in Singapore include the slow loris. The slow loris, a relative of monkeys, is notable for being one of the few mammals that is venomous.

Singapore is also home to pangolins, which are also known as scaly anteaters. These unusual creatures are covered in scales made of keratin, the material that fingernails are made of. During the day, they roll up in a protective ball, and at night they hunt for insects.

Birdlife

Many different kinds of birds make Singapore their home. Herons and egrets wade through shallow water, searching for food, while plovers run along beaches and mudflats, gobbling up insects.

Woodpeckers, warblers, and flycatchers fill the forests. More unusual birds, such as long-tailed parakeets, are also found in the woodlands. These bright green birds live in groups of twenty or more. They have red faces and thin, bluish tail feathers.

Many birds of prey thrive in Singapore, including Brahminy kites, white-bellied sea eagles, and peregrine falcons. Singapore is also home to the osprey, one of the world's more impressive birds of prey. It is a striking creature, usually with a light-colored chest and head in stark contrast to its dark wings. Ospreys are efficient hunters, with a diet that consists almost entirely of fish. As such, it can live in a broad range of habitats

The baya weaver is one of many bird species native to Singapore. Baya weavers build elaborate nests, often over water to help keep predators away.

An osprey carries away a fish it has snatched from the water. Unlike many birds, ospreys can dive all the way underwater when they are hunting.

as long as it is close enough to water to obtain a steady supply of food. The average osprey can spot a fish from 100 feet (30 m) above the water. It will then dive down and hover just above its prey for a moment before snatching it.

Reptiles

Geckos are among the most common reptiles found in Singapore. Many of these small lizards share houses with humans. The nation is also home to large lizards such as monitors, many kinds of turtles, and fearsome crocodiles.

Singapore is also home to one of the most dreaded creatures in the world—the king cobra. Even people who don't fear snakes in general are cautious about cobras. A single bite packs enough venom to kill thirty adults. For a venomous species, it is remarkably large—adults 15 feet (4.6 m) in length are not unusual—and it is quite aggressive when angered. It spreads its hood when it feels threatened, and it rarely backs down from a fight. The king cobra is perhaps the most intelligent of all snake species. For example, when a mother king cobra lays eggs, she digs out a multichambered nest and then protects it, a behavior virtually unknown among snakes. The king cobra can thrive in a variety of habitats. In Singapore, it has learned to live near humans, but it still prefers the relative quiet of forested habitats. Its diet consists primarily of other snakes. When other snakes are not available, the king cobra will eat birds and small mammals instead.

That's a Big One

A common snake in Singapore is also the longest snake in the world. The reticulated python has an average adult length of about 20 feet (6 m), but the longest confirmed was 25 feet 2 inches (7.7 m). The reticulated python is a resident of Singapore and many other parts of Southeast Asia. It prefers to live in wooded areas and rarely strays far from water. The snake swims very well and will often snatch fish or other creatures out of the water to eat. Its diet also includes a variety of mammals and some birds. In Singapore, rats are a major part of its diet. The reticulated python is not venomous. Instead, it kills by constriction—by wrapping itself around its prey and squeezing. It then swallows the prey whole, usually headfirst. Shy but ill tempered, the reticulated python will stand its ground if threatened.

CHAPTER 4

Past and Present

I T IS LIKELY THERE WERE HUMANS LIVING MORE THAN two thousand years ago in the area known today as Singapore. The earliest written record of human habitation in the region comes from around the second century CE.

Changing Hands

Singapore has been a center of trade and commerce since its earliest history. Travelers from China, India, Indonesia, and other lands mentioned it in their records.

Singapore became an important part of Srivijaya, an empire that flourished from the 600s to the 1200s. Srivijaya, which was based on the island of Sumatra, now part of Indonesia, controlled international trade in the region. As an important trading city, Singapore sometimes suffered raids as different groups vied with Srivijaya for power. For example, forces from the Chola kingdom in India attacked the island in 1025 and again later that century.

During the 1300s, Singapore experienced difficult times. It was trapped between warring factions that were vying for control of the Malay Peninsula. The Majapahit kingdom, centered in Java, an island in what is now Indonesia, eventually gained control of Singapore. But this rule didn't last for long, as the island soon fell under the control of the Sultanate of Malacca, based on the Malay Peninsula. In time, Malacca's influence over the island waned, and forces from the European nation of Portugal overran Malacca in the early 1500s. Although ships continued to stop at the island, for the next two centuries Singapore did not hold the same degree of importance in terms of trading and commerce.

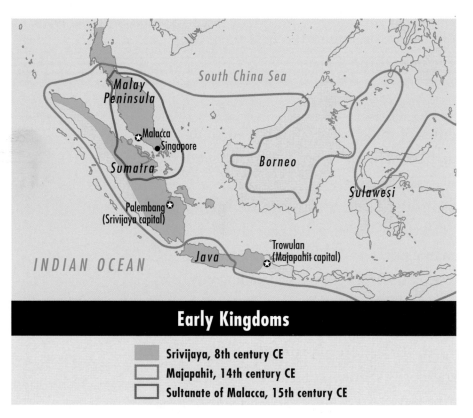

Early Kingdoms

- Srivijaya, 8th century CE
- Majapahit, 14th century CE
- Sultanate of Malacca, 15th century CE

The fourteenth-century gate from Majapahit Palace still stands on the island of Java in Indonesia.

St. John's Island

St. John's is one of the many islands that lie off of Singapore's southern coast. Although it is beautiful land with sandy beaches and palm trees, it also has a dark history. From the late 1800s until about 1939, when World War II began, it was a quarantine station to prevent people suffering from serious infectious diseases from spreading the illnesses to others. Immigrants suspected of having cholera—a disease characterized by stomach pains and vomiting, common in Southeast Asia at the time—were kept there, as were people with smallpox and leprosy. After World War II, the island was repurposed as a prison colony. Finally, in the 1970s, its disturbing legacy was brushed aside when it was given new life as a vacation retreat, a status it maintains to this day. Some of the housing from earlier times still stand, however (left).

The Beginning of Modern Singapore

The Singapore that exists today arose from British interest in the region. By the early 1800s, trade between China and the parts of India controlled by the British Empire had grown extremely valuable. The leaders of the East India Company, which controlled British trade in the region, determined that the waterways around the southern end of the Malay Peninsula were critical to further improving the trade relationship between Britain and Southeast Asia. It would be to East India Company's benefit to establish a powerful influence in the region.

Workers unload tea from ships at the East India Company's docks in London, England. The company controlled the tea trade through much of the nineteenth century.

Dutch trading ships, which often visited Singaporean shores

Sir Thomas Raffles, a merchant working for the East India Company, sailed into the area in order to establish a British presence there. The Dutch had the greatest influence in the region near the Malay Peninsula, and Raffles was instructed not to interfere in any areas that the Dutch occupied. Raffles discovered that the island at the southern tip of the peninsula was free of Dutch influence. At the time, this land was occupied by a few Chinese farmers and some

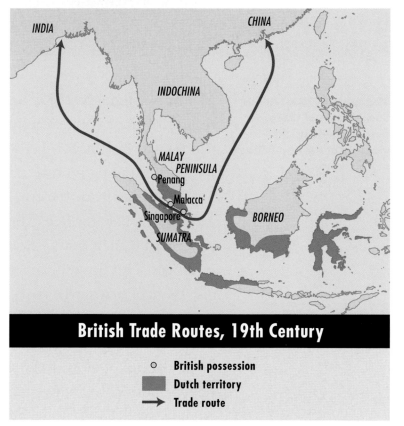

British Trade Routes, 19th Century

- ○ British possession
- ■ Dutch territory
- → Trade route

Singapore in 1830. At this time, people of Chinese descent made up the majority of the population of the island.

Malays. In January 1819, he offered local leaders money in return for their cooperation to establish a British port along the Straits of Malacca—perhaps the most important waterway for British trading routes.

Raffles also made the crucial decision to allow other travelers into the port for free. The Dutch, meanwhile, charged for passage into their ports, so sailors headed for the British port in droves. This not only increased trade at the British port but also brought new settlers to Singapore. The island's population began to grow rapidly. In the early 1820s, a new agreement between Singaporean locals and the British Empire gave the latter control of most of the island. In 1826, Singapore joined Penang and Malacca, two regions in what is now Malaysia, in what was called the Straits Settlements. As the British worked to make their new colonial holding as profitable as possible, modern Singapore began to take shape.

Growing and Changing

In the decades after the British established themselves in the region, Singapore's population increased. The city grew, and its industries developed. Soon, traders were sailing in from all directions—China, India, the Arabian Peninsula. In 1880 alone, more than 1.5 million tons of goods passed through Singapore.

The Founder of Singapore

Thomas Raffles was destined to be a traveler. He had British parents but was born on a ship just off the coast of Jamaica, in the Caribbean Sea, in July 1781. He was a bright boy who worked hard in school and landed a job as a clerk for the British East India Company when he was fourteen years old. Ten years later he went to Southeast Asia—during a time when the British were trying to expand their empire.

He arrived in Singapore in early 1819 and established a British trading post at the very tip of the Malay Peninsula. He also befriended many of the local leaders in the area. After gradually earning their trust, he convinced them to ally themselves with the British rather than with the Dutch, who had already established a presence in the region. Raffles established ports, schools, and churches.

He left Singapore later in 1819 but returned again to govern the island in 1822 and 1823. During this time, he helped write the first constitution for Singapore. The following year, he returned to England, where he died in 1826.

Giving Back

One of the most important figures in the development of modern Singapore was Gan Eng Seng. He was born into a poor family in 1844 in what is now the nation of Malaysia. Gan had very little education as a child because he had to work to help support his family. But he was smart, diligent, and hardworking. Following his father's death in 1860, he began working for a Malaysian farming company named Guthrie. He moved to Singapore and rose swiftly through the Guthrie ranks, remaining with them for many years as he developed a keen sense for business.

Gan never forgot the struggle of having a limited education, and he dreamed of one day establishing a school for those who could not afford it. In 1885, he achieved this dream when he opened the Anglo-Chinese Free School, which later became known as the Gan Eng Seng School (GESS). Children enrolled in droves, and within five years the Singaporean government was supporting it with public funds. Within ten years, Gan was able to oversee the opening of more locations. He died in 1899 at age fifty-five. GESS is now one of the oldest educational institutions in Singapore.

By the 1880s, Singapore had become an important trading center, and its economy was growing quickly.

British leaders, however, were unprepared for the explosion of population and business, and many ordinary citizens suffered from a lack of food, clean water, and services. There was little law enforcement, and underground activities such as gambling and the drug trade thrived. By the end of the 1800s, the British government was addressing many of these problems, but with limited success.

The majority of people on the island by this time were Chinese. Many Chinese people fled their homeland during periods of political upheaval. By the early 1900s, some had gathered to form a united revolutionary front in the hope of creating a better China. That dream became a reality in 1911 with the Xinhai Revolution, which resulted in the overthrow of the Qing Dynasty and the establishment of the Republic of China.

By the beginning of the twentieth century, the European neighborhoods of Singapore were filled with large, stately buildings and horse-drawn carriages.

British ships patrol the waters around Singapore in the months leading up to World War II.

Despite Singapore's proximity to busy ocean routes, it was little affected by the events of World War I (1914–1918). When the war ended, the British, nervous from rumors that the Japanese leadership might want to overrun the island, began building a large naval base there, which was completed in 1939. By this time, trouble was brewing around the globe. Soon, World War II would begin, and it would have a much more profound effect on Singapore than the previous world war had.

Japan Moves In

World War II began in Europe in 1939, and over the next two years it expanded to include much of the globe. In the war, the Allies, led by Great Britain, the United States, and the Soviet Union, were fighting the Axis powers, led by Germany, Italy, and Japan.

In early December 1941, Japanese forces landed on the Malay Peninsula. The British and their allies did not have enough troops, equipment, or weapons to stop the invasion. Japanese forces moved south down the peninsula, and in less than two months they could see Singapore. The Allied powers attempted to repel the Japanese by destroying bridges to the island, but the Japanese invaded using boats instead in

Singapore smolders following a Japanese air raid in February 1942. The Battle of Singapore lasted a week. By its end, Japanese forces controlled the island.

February 1942. After a brief period of intense fighting, the Allies, exhausted and outgunned, were forced to surrender, and the Japanese took control of the island. For the next three and a half years, the people of Singapore suffered unimaginable horrors. Chinese people received the harshest treatment. Many of those who were identified as having played a role in supporting resistance to the Japanese in China were executed. Some experts estimate that the death toll was as high as fifty thousand.

Singaporeans wait in line to vote in 1959, the year Singapore became self-governing.

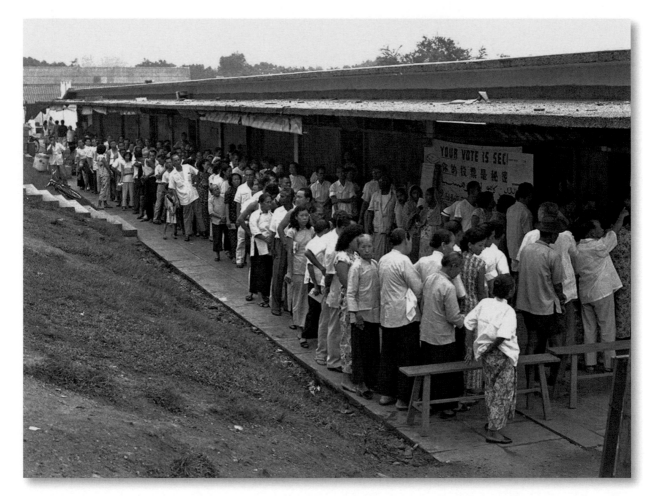

The war ended when Japan fell to Allied forces in 1945. Although Singapore reverted to British rule, the Singaporeans wanted change. Their resentment at Britain's inability to protect them from Japanese brutality inspired feelings of nationalism, and by the 1950s Singapore was on its way to becoming a truly independent nation.

Calling Their Own Shots

In 1959, Singapore became self-governing. The nation held public elections for its own government, made up of its own citizens. Britain, however, continued to be responsible for Singapore's defense and foreign policy.

In 1963, Singapore joined neighboring states to form the federation of Malaysia. Singapore's leaders had been concerned about joining Malaysia primarily out of concern for Singapore's small size and lack of natural resources. It was a troubled relationship, however. Racial tensions between Malays and Singaporeans of Chinese descent resulted in riots. In 1965, the Malaysian government forced Singapore out of Malaysia.

In recent decades, the manufacture of pharmaceuticals, or medicines, has become a major industry in Singapore.

Recent Times

Once again on its own, Singapore began expanding relationships with other nations beyond its closest neighbors. It also began aggressive policies to broaden its industrial base. It used its tax laws to lure investors and increase manufacturing. Beginning in 1971, when Great Britain ended its military defense of Singapore, the young nation also had to form and staff its own military.

In the 1980s, Singapore's business and government leaders embraced emerging technology developments, well before many of their Asian peers. They also invested in local infrastructure improvements to roads, housing, and public transportation. In the years after, the government continued to make policy that helped business. In 2003, Singapore signed a free trade agreement with the United States. This agreement eliminated import and export taxes on goods traded between the two nations. Although

Singapore had a strong economy, in 2008 it suffered an economic downturn during a worldwide economic recession. The nation did not recover until about 2010. At that time, tourism began to grow, in part because Singapore legalized casino gambling and opened two large casino resorts, attracting many visitors.

In recent decades, as Singapore has modernized it has surpassed the progress of other nations. By expanding its economy, carefully managing its resources, and protecting its environment, Singapore has become one of the most prosperous nations in all of Asia.

Cranes rise from the towers of the Marina Bay Sands resort. A combination hotel, casino, shopping center, and convention center, the resort opened in 2010.

CHAPTER 5

Governing the City-State

THE STRUCTURE AND ACTIVITY OF SINGAPORE'S government is based on its constitution, which took effect on August 9, 1965. This document became the blueprint for the nation's independence that continues to this day. Singapore's government is divided into three branches, or parts: executive, legislative, and judicial. Each has its own area of responsibility.

Executive Branch

The executive branch of any government bears the responsibility of carrying out laws and other policies. In Singapore, those responsibilities fall to the president and the cabinet. The president is elected by the people to a six-year term. Singaporean citizens must be twenty-one years old to vote. The cabinet is a group of ministers who head various governmental departments, such as finance, education, foreign affairs, and environment and water resources. The cabinet members are under the leadership of the prime minister. Unlike in the

United States where the president is the head of government, Singapore's head of government is the prime minister. The president of Singapore can veto, or reject, certain appointments and other decisions, but the position is largely ceremonial. The president is sometimes involved in drafting new legislation, but the cabinet has the final say about the new law. The president does not have the power to veto new legislation. Tony Tan became president in 2011. Previously, he had been a member of the parliament for twenty-seven years.

An honor guard greets President Tony Tan during a National Day parade, which celebrates Singapore's independence from Malaysia in 1965.

The National Government of Singapore

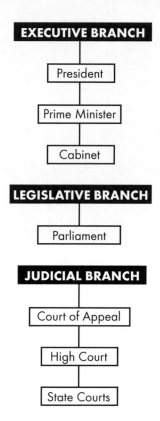

EXECUTIVE BRANCH

President

Prime Minister

Cabinet

LEGISLATIVE BRANCH

Parliament

JUDICIAL BRANCH

Court of Appeal

High Court

State Courts

The prime minister has significant power over both the president and the rest of the cabinet. Under Singapore's constitution, the prime minister can assign each minister whatever tasks are necessary, even if it is outside the scope of that minister's department. The prime minister can also create, merge, or eliminate departments. The prime minister is almost always in the political party that holds the most seats in parliament.

Lee Hsien Loong (above right) has been prime minister since 2004. He is the country's third prime minister.

Legislative Branch

The legislative, or lawmaking, branch of Singapore's government consists of the parliament. Unlike the U.S. Congress, which has two chambers, the Senate and the House of Representatives, the Singapore Parliament is unicameral, meaning it has just one chamber. Singapore's parliament has 101 members. Of those, 89 are elected. The remaining members are appointed.

The leader of Singapore's parliament is called the Speaker. Another important figure in parliament is the leader of the opposition, who leads debates for the political party with the second most members. Any given parliament can last for a maximum of five years. After that time, the parliament is dissolved, and elections for new members are held within ninety days of the dissolution.

The primary function of the Singapore Parliament is to create new laws or amend, or change, existing laws. Committees are formed to study legal issues, forge new language, and participate in debates. Aside from lawmaking, the parliament controls most of the nation's financial matters.

Judicial Branch

Singapore's judicial system consists of two tiers. The top tier is called the Supreme Court, while the lower tier is called the state courts. The Supreme Court is made up of two bodies—

Leading the Nation

Of the many celebrated political leaders Singapore has had, few were more admired than Lee Kuan Yew. Born in 1923, Yew was fourth-generation Singaporean. He was raised speaking English and later learned both Chinese and Japanese, the latter during World War II so he could act as a translator. He entered politics in 1954. At that time, he and a group of colleagues formed the People's Action Party (PAP), which remains the dominant political party in Singapore to this day. Lee Kuan Yew became Singapore's first prime minister in 1959. He held that position during and after Singapore's merging with Malaysia, until 1990. During that time, he was at the center of landmark decisions on countless matters, including anticorruption law, management of natural resources, and national security. No one was more important in shaping the Singapore that exists today. He died in 2015 at the age of ninety-one.

the High Court and the Court of Appeal. The Court of Appeal is the highest court in the land. It reviews decisions made in lower courts. The High Court both hears appeals from lower courts and tries important cases. These include major lawsuits and criminal cases in which the defendant faces more than ten years in prison or the death penalty. Judges on these courts are appointed by the president on the recommendation of the prime minister.

State courts handle lesser offenses. The president appoints the judges on these courts on the recommendation of the chief justice. Unlike the United States, Singapore does not use jury trials. Instead, all trials are heard by a judge.

The National Flag

The flag of Singapore is simple in design, but full of symbolism. It features two colors—red and white. The bottom half of the flag is white, while the top is red. On the left side of the red band is a white crescent moon with five white stars next to it. According to Singaporean tradition, red stands for equality and harmony among all people, and white symbolizes purity and integrity. The crescent moon is a metaphor for the nation itself, which is still relatively young, yet is always rising and progressing. And the stars represent the five principles that guide the nation's people—progress, justice, harmony, democracy, and equality. The flag was first adopted in December 1959, when Singapore was a self-ruling nation but still under the governance of the British Empire. When Singapore became fully independent in 1965, the flag was officially readopted, although no changes were made to its appearance.

Statutory Boards

The Singaporean government also includes statutory boards. These are smaller governmental bodies, like agencies in the United States, that are overseen by a cabinet ministry. Although a ministry manages each board, the boards function largely on their own, without interference from the ministries. Each board has a clear purpose. For example, the Economic Development Board studies and recommends ways for Singapore to remain one of the global leaders in commerce. The board determines ways to provide job opportunities to its citizens and to create investment incentives for foreigners.

Singapore's High Court and Court of Appeal are located in a disc-shaped building that opened in 2005.

Supporters of the People's Action Party cheer on their candidates in 2015.

Political Parties

Unlike the United States, which has two main political parties, Singapore has one predominant party, called the People's Action Party (PAP). The PAP has nearly complete control of the government. For example, in 2015, the PAP won eighty-three of the eighty-nine elected parliamentary seats.

The PAP was formed in 1959 and has dominated the Singaporean government ever since. The PAP tends to favor the needs of business. While there is little doubt that Singapore's economic development since 1959 has been remarkable, the PAP has also been criticized for restricting civil liberties. The PAP has tried to silence its political opposition by controlling the press and restricting free speech.

A Look at the City

Singapore is a nation and a city. In 2014, it had a population of about 5,487,000. Although Singapore is one large city, it is a very clean, green, and livable one. Ten percent of the land is devoted to parks and nature reserves. People enjoy the carefully tended gardens at the Singapore Botanic Gardens. They can also explore the wilds of the Bukit Timah Nature Reserve, which protects an ancient rain forest. Even without going to such sites, people in Singapore can feel like they are near nature. Wooded paths connect many of the city's parks, and trees line the roads. One of the most popular sites is Gardens by the Bay (second photo below), which features vertical gardens growing up huge iron structures shaped like trees.

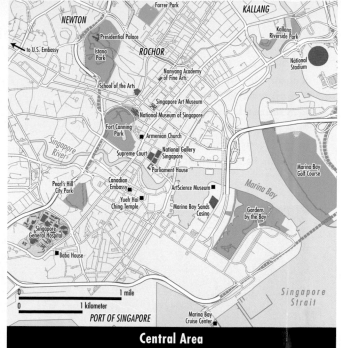

Central Area

Singapore is a mix of gleaming modern buildings, such as the Esplanade performing arts center, and modest buildings from another time. The Baba House is a well-preserved example of how a wealthy Chinese family would have lived in the nineteenth century. Today, most Singaporeans live in high-rise apartment buildings.

The highest concentration of skyscrapers is in a region called the Central Area. It is the commercial and financial heart of the nation. It is also a historic area, with some of the oldest churches and temples in Singapore. The Armenian Church, for instance, built in the 1830s, is the oldest church in Singapore. The neighborhood also boasts the Yueh Hai Ching Temple, one of the oldest Daoist temples in Singapore.

As an international center of trade and finance, Singapore attracts visitors from all around the world. Many come to do business, but they also enjoy the shopping, the food, and the beaches.

The second most powerful party in Singapore is the Workers' Party, which was founded in 1957. Compared to the PAP, the Workers' Party places more emphasis on the needs of everyday citizens. Today, it has just a handful of representatives in the parliament.

National Anthem

The national anthem of Singapore is "Majulah Singapura" ("Onward Singapore"). It was written in 1958 by Zubir Said. Originally, it was intended only for City Council of Singapore functions. The following year, when Singapore became self-governing, it was adopted as the national anthem.

Malay lyrics	**English lyrics**
Mari kita rakyat Singapura	Come, fellow Singaporeans
Sama-sama menuju bahagia	Let us progress towards happiness together
Cita-cita kita yang mulia	May our noble aspiration bring
Berjaya Singapura	Singapore success
Marilah kita bersatu	Come, let us unite
Dengan semangat yang baru	In a new spirit
Semua kita berseru	Together we proclaim
Majulah Singapura	Onward Singapore
Majulah Singapura	Onward Singapore
Marilah kita bersatu	Come, let us unite
Dengan semangat yang baru	In a new spirit
Semua kita berseru	Together we proclaim
Majulah Singapura	Onward Singapore
Majulah Singapura	Onward Singapore

CHAPTER 6

A Powerful Economy

SINGAPORE BOASTS ONE OF THE MOST IMPRESSIVE economies in all of Asia, and one of the strongest in the world. It has a relatively high average income per person and one of the lowest unemployment rates of any country in the world. Less than 2 percent of people who want to work do not have a job. People from other countries remain interested in investing in Singapore, and Singapore remains committed to exploring new business ventures.

If the nation's economy has a weak spot, it lies in the fact that Singapore is dependent upon imports from other nations for many basic necessities, including oil, gas, many food items, and clean water. Nevertheless, the average Singaporean has a job that pays well, a safe and clean place to live, a means of transportation, reliable health care, and some money left over for a little fun. In short, the quality of life is good, and there are many career opportunities for people who like to work hard.

Opposite: **About one hundred thousand people in Singapore work in the construction industry.**

A Little History

Singapore's economic outlook was not always so bright. When Singapore left Malaysia in 1965 and became truly independent, many of its citizens were living in terrible conditions. Money was in short supply, and the unemployment rate was in the mid-teens. Crime was increasing, and many people felt fearful and uncertain about the future.

Fortunately, the government took immediate action and formed a plan to improve the nation's economy. Singapore

In the 1960s, the streets of Singapore were lined with two- and three-story buildings. Today, highrises dominate the city.

invested in infrastructure improvements such as roads, bridges, and buildings in order to make the nation more attractive to foreign investors. New rules and regulations were enacted with the same purpose—to make the nation as business friendly as possible to investors from other parts of the world. One way Singapore encouraged investment was by offering tax breaks. If a manufacturing company looking to expand into the Asian market built its new plant in Singapore, the company would pay a lower tax rate on items it produced for export than if it built its plant somewhere else. Singapore also invested in its workforce by pouring money into educating and training the population. The government has insisted that most Singaporeans learn the English language, and an English-

More than four out of every five workers in Singapore are employed in service industries.

Most people in Singapore live in apartment complexes that have many appealing features, such as swimming pools.

speaking workforce is attractive to businesspeople in other parts of the world. The government ensured that Singaporean citizens could make themselves more valuable as workers. The well-trained citizens, in turn, became more valuable to the nation, and the nation became more attractive to investors.

The results of the government's actions were remarkable. In one generation, the nation rose out of near-poverty and became one of the most powerful economic forces in Asia. In time, its citizens began to enjoy a higher standard of living and greater financial security than they had ever known. Most of the population moved into the middle class. Over the years, the government has continued its commitment to Singapore remaining one of the most desirable places in the world to live and work.

Working in Singapore

Although Singapore is a small country, it has a sizable workforce. About 3.6 million people go to a job every day. And nonresidents—people from other countries who work in Singapore—account for another 700,000 workers. About two-thirds of the nonresident workers are in relatively unskilled positions such as construction or manufacturing. Another one-third works in business positions such as management.

Both Singaporean and foreign workers have offices in Singapore's many skyscrapers.

Although Singapore offers a lot of job opportunities to foreign workers, the government has policies in place to move nonresident workers out of the country and back to their native lands during times of economic hardship. Other laws can make working in Singapore difficult for foreigners, too. For example, if foreigners get a permit to work in Singapore in a specific job and then after a few months decide they don't like it, they cannot simply move into another position in

Many construction workers in Singapore come from India and Bangladesh.

another company. They have to leave Singapore and go back to their home country. Similarly, if foreigners get fired, their permit to be in Singapore is no longer valid, and they have to go back to their native country within a week. Also, foreign workers who want to marry native Singaporeans must receive special permission to do so from the agency that issued their work permit.

A farmer checks his crops at his family farm in Singapore. Just 1 percent of Singaporean workers are employed in agriculture.

Agriculture

Agriculture makes up a small part of Singapore's economy. The country has little land to use for growing crops, and only about 1 percent of the Singaporean workforce makes a living in agriculture. But some vegetables are raised there, including spinach, cabbage, and lettuce. Coconuts and mushrooms are also grown. The country is an important source for orchids and other decorative plants. Some Singaporeans also raise livestock. There are about 3.5 million chickens and 272,000 pigs in the country.

Some people in Singapore fish for a living. Most of the fish are caught in the sea, but aquaculture—fish farming—is also growing in Singapore. Sea bass, grouper, and prawns are all raised on farms in Singapore.

Manufacturing

Manufacturing makes up a much larger part of the Singaporean economy than agriculture does. It employs about 16 percent of workers. Goods manufactured in Singapore include electronics, medicines, chemicals, and transportation equipment. Singapore also produces processed foods, beverages, rubber products, and drilling and other industrial equipment.

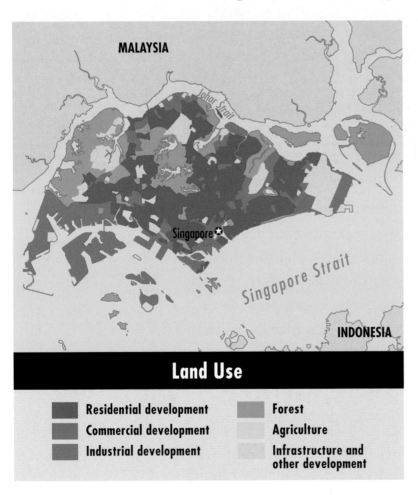

Land Use

Residential development

Commercial development

Industrial development

Forest

Agriculture

Infrastructure and other development

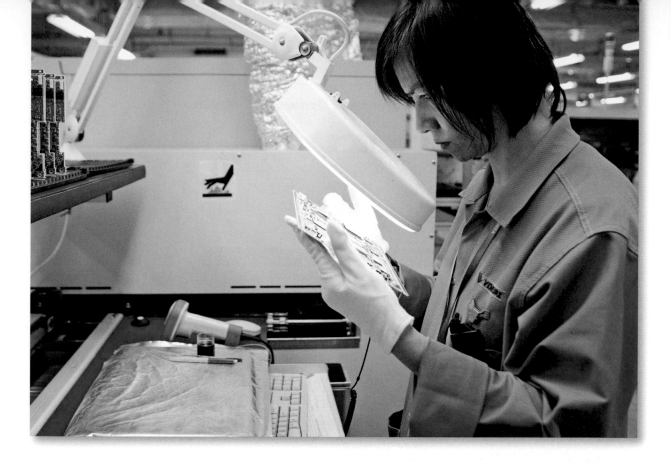

Services

The largest part of Singapore's economy is the service sector. Services account for three-quarters of Singapore's economy and employ more than 80 percent of its workforce. The service sector includes a broad array of businesses, such as banking, telecommunications, health care, and education.

Tourism is a major part of Singapore's service economy. The visitors sleep in hotels, eat in restaurants, travel on trains, and gamble in casinos, all parts of the service sector. About fifteen million foreign visitors arrive in Singapore every year.

Singapore is one of the world's largest banking centers. It is also the third-largest oil refinery center. It has one of the world's busiest ports and is an important site for ship repair.

What Singapore Grows and Makes

AGRICULTURE (2012)

Chickens	3,500,000 birds
Spinach	2,200 metric tons
Orchids	15% of the world market

MANUFACTURING (2012, VALUE ADDED)

Electronic products	US$15,043,000,000
Medicines	US$13,427,000,000
Transportation equipment	US$9,435,000,000

Huge containers filled with cargo are piled high at the port of Singapore. Each container is the size of a semi truck.

Trade

A huge part of Singapore's economic success hinges on its relationships with other nations. It exports more than US$400 billion worth of goods and services each year. Its main trading partners include its close neighbors—Malaysia, China, Hong Kong, Indonesia, Japan, and South Korea—as well as the United States. It has also been fostering relations with the European Union for some time. Goods it exports include heavy industrial equipment, electronics, medicines, and refined petroleum. Singapore imports food, water, and fuels.

Financial companies from around the world have offices in Singapore.

More than 3,000 companies from around the world have put some of their money into Singapore. The United States is one of its biggest investors. Over 1,500 American-owned businesses have some kind of presence in Singapore.

Money Facts

The basic unit of currency in Singapore is the dollar, which is divided into one hundred cents. The Singapore dollar is often abbreviated S$. Singapore produces coins in values of 5, 10, 20, and 50 cents, and 1 dollar. Paper money comes in denominations of 2, 5, 10, 50, 100, 500, and 1,000 dollars. There is also a $10,000 note, but it is rarely used. Each bill has a dominant color. The $2 bill, for instance, is violet, while the $5 is green. All bills show an image of Yusof bin Ishak, the nation's first president, on the front. The back features images of Singaporean life. The reverse of the $2 bill, for example, shows a teacher in front of a group of schoolchildren, as well as several schools and universities. The reverse of the $10 shows athletes in action. Other subjects include arts, government, and economics. In 2015, S$1 equaled US$0.71, and US$1.00 equaled S$1.40.

CHAPTER 7

Diverse People

SINGAPORE IS HOME TO ROUGHLY 5.5 MILLION people, nearly one-third of whom are foreign workers rather than Singaporean citizens. It is an ethnically diverse nation. The largest group, about 74 percent, consists of people of Chinese descent. Another 13 percent of Singaporeans are Malayan, and about 9 percent are Indian. Another 3 percent consists of people of many different backgrounds, predominantly European. This diversity makes Singapore a truly cosmopolitan place.

Getting Along

The people of Singapore are actually much more diverse than appears from these statistics. Singaporeans of Chinese descent trace their origins to many different parts of China, and they speak versions of Chinese that are so different that they can-

Opposite: **During the Christmas season, Orchard Road is filled with shoppers.**

Ethnic Singapore (2013 est.)	
Chinese	74.2%
Malay	13.3%
Indian	9.2%
Other	3.3%

not understand one another. Similarly, most Malays speak the Malay language, but others speak Javanese or Boyanese. Indian Singaporeans come from many different backgrounds. There are Tamils, Malayalis, Pakistanis, Sinhalese, and more.

Although there are ethnic neighborhoods in Singapore, the nation puts a tremendous emphasis on racial harmony. The government works to encourage everyone to get along. There is, for example, a national holiday called Racial Harmony Day, which is celebrated on July 21. Its primary purpose is to remind the people of Singapore of the tragic

Two women of Malay descent walk near a mosque in Singapore. Most Malays in Singapore are Muslim.

Chinese signs hang from buildings in Singapore's Chinatown. Although the neighborhood retains a cultural connection to its Chinese history, it is actually a diverse area.

riots that occurred in 1964 between Chinese and Malay Singaporeans, which resulted in thirty-six deaths and more than 550 injuries. The holiday also serves as a way to experience the variety of cultural identities present in Singapore, encouraging people to celebrate their backgrounds and differences. In schools, for example, students wear costumes and give presentations and performances that underscore their cultural heritage. Sometimes they also play games and enjoy foods that arise from their ancestry.

Even though the people of Singapore have diverse backgrounds, most citizens think of themselves as Singaporeans first and their ethnic heritage second. This plays a role in creating a relatively harmonious society.

British workers in Singapore relax at a British-style pub.

Many Languages

Just as Singapore is a place of tremendous ethnic diversity, it is also a place where diverse languages are spoken. English, Mandarin Chinese, Malay, and Tamil are all official languages. In Singapore, some signs are only in English. Many, however, are in all four languages.

English is the language of business and government. The English used in Singapore is the English spoken and written in Great Britain. Singaporean English uses the British spellings. For example, in Singapore, the words *color*, *harbor*, and *theater* are spelled *colour*, *harbour*, and *theatre*.

Mandarin Chinese is the most common of several Chinese languages spoken in Singapore. Other Chinese languages used in Singapore include Hokkien, Teochew, and Cantonese. Chinese does not have an alphabet. Instead, it uses characters, each of which stands for a word or a syllable. To be fluent in Chinese, a person needs to know about three thousand characters.

Malay is an important ceremonial language in Singapore. It is usually the language of choice for Singapore's national

The most common language of newspapers in Singapore is English. The second most common is Chinese.

Malay is one of Singapore's four official languages. In addition to Singapore, it is also the official language of Malaysia, Indonesia, and Brunei. Here are a few words and phrases in the Malay language:

Ya	Yes
Tidak	No
Selamat pagi	Good morning
Selamat tinggal	Good-bye (said if you're leaving)
Selamat jalan	Good-bye (said if you're staying)
Semoga hari anda baik sahaja.	Have a nice day.
Berapa harganya ini?	How much is this?
Terima kasih	Thank you

anthem. It is also important because of Singapore's proximity with Malaysia, where it is the official language. In Singapore, the Malay language is written in the Latin alphabet, the same alphabet that is used to write English.

A warning sign is written in Singapore's four major languages: English, Chinese, Malay, and Tamil.

DANGER-KEEP OUT !
危险，请避开！
BAHAYA-JANGAN DEKAT !
அபாயம்-அருகில் வராதீர்கள் !

Tamil is a language that arose farther west in Asia. It is spoken in Sri Lanka and in parts of India. In the Tamil language, there are twelve vowels and eighteen consonants. It uses a flowing script that incorporates many curved letters.

The government encourages its citizens to be multilingual. It is considered beneficial to a nation that has robust relationships with so many other nations. Just about all Singaporean children can speak at least two languages fluently. In school, children are taught English as their primary language, but then they are also taught a second language, called the mother tongue. Which language this is varies from school to school. For example, Mandarin is often the mother tongue in areas with large Chinese populations.

Singaporean Indians belong to many different ethnic groups, including Tamils, Punjabis, and Bengalis.

Inside the Numbers

Singapore has a relatively young population, with the average age being about thirty-four. Singapore is also a very healthy place, with one of the highest life expectancies of anywhere in the world. Men in Singapore live an average of eighty-two years and women an average of eighty-seven years. In the United

About 9 percent of Singaporeans are at least sixty-five years of age.

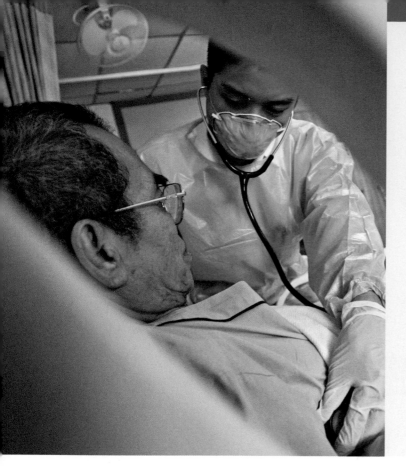

Singapore has one of the most efficient and effective health care systems in the world. The great majority of citizens get their coverage through a public health system managed by the government. The money that supports the plan comes from a mixture of two sources—contributions from people's paychecks and subsidies from the government. All medical treatment in Singapore requires patients to pay something when they visit doctors, although the cost of basic care such as checkups is quite reasonable. The value of this approach is that it discourages people from getting unnecessary tests and treatments. Not everyone in Singapore can take advantage of the health care system. Many of the benefits enjoyed by residents are not available to people from other countries who are there on work permits.

States, by comparison, men typically live to be seventy-seven years old and women eighty-two. Singapore also has one of the lowest infant mortality rates in the world. This is the number of babies that die before reaching their first birthday. In Singapore, the infant mortality rate is just 2.5. The rate in the United States is more than twice as high, at 6.2.

In part, Singapore's healthy population is the result of its excellent health care system. According to the World Health Organization, Singapore has the sixth-best health care system in the world. There are large numbers of doctors and dentists, and the government helps pay for health care so that everyone can afford it.

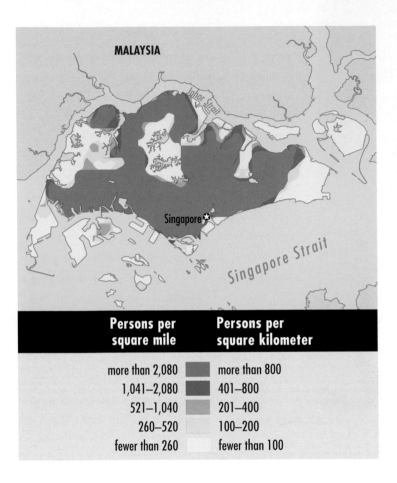

MALAYSIA

Johor Strait

Singapore ✪

Singapore Strait

Persons per square mile	**Persons per square kilometer**
more than 2,080	more than 800
1,041–2,080	401–800
521–1,040	201–400
260–520	100–200
fewer than 260	fewer than 100

Singapore is a fairly crowded place, with an average of about 7,700 people living on every square mile (about 3,000 people per sq km) of land. This makes it one of the most densely populated countries on earth. In order for there to be room for so many people to live on such a small area of land, housing consists mainly of high-rise apartment buildings.

Education

Singapore has one of the best education systems in Southeast Asia. The government has shown a great commitment to improving its schools and maintaining high standards. About one-fifth of the country's annual budget is spent on education. Most schools are public, but there are many private schools as well. Parents also have the option of sending their children to religious schools or homeschooling them. They must get permission from the government, however. Children are required by law to be enrolled in primary school, and failure to do so can result in heavy fines for the parents. Once children are enrolled, they must maintain solid attendance records. Failure to do so can also result in fines for the parents.

The Singaporean public school system is structured a little differently than that in the United States. Young children attend preschool and kindergarten. Primary school starts at about age seven and covers grades one through six. In primary school, students study English, another language, math, science, moral education, civics, arts and crafts, health, music, and more.

Colorful apartment buildings in Singapore. Although most Singaporeans do not have private yards, most apartment complexes have pleasant grounds where people can relax, and the city is filled with parks.

After primary school is secondary school, which starts over with grades one through five. At this point, a student is finished with the American equivalent of high school. In high school, many students learn a third language. Sometimes this is a second mother tongue. Other times it is a foreign language such as French, German, or Japanese.

Children at public schools in Singapore are required to wear uniforms.

In order to attend a college or university, a student must first complete a test known as an O-level exam. This helps administrators determine a student's abilities and qualifications. There is a tremendous number of educational venues for students, including junior colleges, polytechnics, universities, and technical institutes. The two largest universities in Singapore are the National University of Singapore and Nanyang Technological University. Each serves more than thirty thousand students.

Students at Singapore Polytechnic relax between classes. The school educates students in fields such as engineering, information technology, and nursing.

CHAPTER 8

The Spiritual World

百龍寶殿

SINGAPORE IS ONE OF THE MOST RELIGIOUSLY diverse nations in the world, and probably the single most diverse country in Southeast Asia. The government's strong emphasis on tolerance of all faiths has both attracted people to Singapore and kept religious conflicts to a minimum.

Opposite: **A Buddhist temple in Singapore**

Buddhism

The most commonly practiced religion in Singapore is Buddhism. About one-third of the Singaporean population adheres to it. The Buddhist faith does not follow a belief in a god or gods. Instead, it follows the teachings of Siddhartha Gautama, a thinker and philosopher who lived in eastern India sometime around the fifth century BCE. He is more commonly known as the Buddha, which means the "enlightened

Religion in Singapore (2010 est.)	
Buddhist	33%
Christian	18%
Muslim	15%
Daoist	11%
Hindu	5%
Other	1%
None	17%

one." Buddhists attempt to attain inner peace by overcoming ignorance and the desire for worldly things. It is this desire, the Buddha taught, that ultimately leads to suffering. Buddhism has three main schools, or branches—Theravada, Mahayana, and Vajrayana. All three are popular in Singapore.

Christianity

The second most common faith in Singapore is Christianity. About 18 percent of the nation's population is Christian. Christianity is, in fact, the largest religion in the world, with nearly

A Buddhist man prays at a temple in Singapore. Buddhists do not believe in a creator god, so they do not pray to one. For many Buddhists, prayer is more like meditation.

2.5 billion followers. The fundamental principles of Christianity include the belief that there is one true God, and that Christians should follow the teachings of God's son, the wholly human Jesus Christ, whose life is described in the Bible's New Testament. There are many different versions of Christianity. The largest is Roman Catholicism. Roughly one-third of the Christians who live in Singapore are Catholic. The other two-thirds follow one of the many Protestant denominations, including Anglicanism, Lutheranism, Methodism, and Pentecostalism. The vast majority of Christians in Singapore are of Chinese descent. Many Singaporean Christians are well versed in the traditions and practices of other faiths. In fact, some smaller churches follow basic Christian principles but have also adopted elements of other faiths, creating a hybrid denomination.

St. Andrew's Cathedral is the largest Anglican church in Singapore.

Singapore's Sultan Mosque. Muslims pray at specific times during the day, which change depending on the sunrise and sunset. Mosques typically include a minaret, a tall tower that broadcasts the call to prayer.

Islam

Islam is also widely practiced in Singapore. The Muslim faith is based on the teachings of Muhammad, who lived from about 570 to 632 CE. Muslims believe that Muhammad received messages from God, and that he was the last of God's prophets. The messages were said to have been collected into the Qur'an, the text that forms the basis of Islam. Like Christians, Muslims believe there is only one God, the same god that Christians worship. There are three main branches of Islam in Singapore: Sunni, Shia, and Ahmadi. Sunni is the most commonly observed. Almost all Singaporeans of Malay ethnicity are Muslim, as is about one-quarter of the Indian population.

Daoism

Daoism, which began in China more than two thousand years ago, is also popular in Singapore. It began with the work of Laozi, an author, poet, and philosopher. Daoism encourages people to live harmoniously with the forces that exist all around them. One of the philosophies most associated with Daoism is that of yin and yang, forces that are seemingly opposite but in fact are mutually beneficial and interconnected. About 10 percent of the population of Singapore practices Daoism.

Laozi may have lived in the sixth century BCE. Many historians do not believe that the writings attributed to him were written by one person.

Hinduism

About 5 percent of Singaporeans follow Hinduism. The Hindu faith is the third largest in the world, after Christianity and Islam, and is the most common religion in India. Although the Hindu presence in Singapore can be traced back to ancient Srivijaya, the great majority of Hindus in Singapore trace their roots back to Indian migrants who came to Singapore in the early 1800s. Hindu practices come in many different forms, and for many Hindus it is more a life

Sri Mariamman Temple is the oldest Hindu temple in Singapore. It is decorated with dozens of sculptures of Hindu deities.

Singaporean girls take
part in a Hindu service.

philosophy than the worship of any single god. Hindus generally believe that one must search for truth in many different ways. They consider tolerance, honesty, and patience among the highest virtues.

Governmental Policies

Although the people of Singapore have freedom of religion, the government does place some limits on people's religious rights. The government reserves the right, for example, to censor some religious publications and prohibit forums for public discussion of religious beliefs. If, for example, people wanted to speak publicly against a particular religion, they

Singaporean girls take
part in a Hindu service.

Religious Holidays

No one religion dominates in Singapore. The important holidays from all the major religions represented in the country are national holidays. The dates of many of these holidays vary from year to year.

Good Friday	Christian, crucifixion of Jesus Christ
Vesak Day	Buddhist, Buddha's birthday
Deepavali	Hindu, Festival of Lights
Christmas	Christian, birth of Jesus Christ
Hari Raya Puasa	Muslim, end of Ramadan
Hari Raya Haji	Muslim, Feast of Sacrifice

would be at risk of arrest, fines, and imprisonment. The government also discourages religious groups and influential religious figures from taking part in political activities. This is because it is national policy that all religions should be equal to one another in the country. By attempting to gain greater political influence or the power to affect the political process, religious leaders also risk offending members of other faiths.

The Singaporean government has taken a hard-line position against one particular religious group—the Jehovah's Witnesses. In Singapore, every religion needs to be formally recognized by the government through a registration process, and in 1972 the government revoked that registration for the Jehovah's Witnesses and outlawed the faith. The reasoning was that the Jehovah's Witnesses followed practices that threatened public interest and disrupted harmony among religions. For example, the Jehovah's Witnesses do not believe in participation in military service, yet in Singapore every male is required to serve at least one term in the military. Jehovah's Witnesses also do not swear an oath to any nation or salute a nation's flag.

Citizens caught worshipping as Jehovah's Witnesses or in possession of any Jehovah's Witnesses literature, such as their publication *The Watchtower*, can face heavy fines or jail time. Nonetheless, about a thousand Jehovah's Witnesses live in Singapore, and the government has only rarely taken action against them. If a group of Jehovah's Witnesses worships in the home of one of its members, for example, the government does not interfere.

In Singapore, people can be arrested for speaking against religions. In 2015, a teenager named Amos Yee (center) was sentenced to four weeks in prison for posting a video online that was considered offensive to Christians.

CHAPTER 9

Arts and Sports

AS WITH SO MANY OTHER ASPECTS OF LIFE IN Singapore, the government plays a significant role in the arts. While the government does encourage its artists to express themselves, it sets boundaries that it prefers they work within. The government must also review and approve art before it is publicly displayed.

Singapore has a unique term that is used when discussing what's acceptable to be mentioned in public: *OB marker*. It stands for "out of bounds." Government officials use the term when talking about what is appropriate. OB markers can change depending on issues such as who is in political power, the overall mood of the nation at a given time, and the state of a relationship between Singapore and another country. Political topics are generally discouraged, as is material that is religiously or ethnically charged. Still, if artists are willing to stick to topics that are considered safe, they are then free to do pretty much as they like.

Opposite: **Chinese musical traditions are strong in Singapore. Here, a man plays a pipa, a stringed instrument that developed in China.**

The Singapore Art Museum displays contemporary art from Singapore and elsewhere around Southeast Asia.

Visual Arts

The Singaporean leadership has made a strong effort in recent decades to include a robust art scene in its sophisticated city. Artists are encouraged to bring their best pieces to Singapore for exhibition and sale. Fairs and other events such as Art Stage Singapore, the Affordable Art Fair, and the Singapore Biennale provide thousands of artists a chance to showcase their works to potential buyers. Similarly, the establishment of the Singapore Art Museum in the 1990s signaled greater government support for the arts. This support continued with the opening of the National Gallery Singapore in 2015.

Singapore is also taking steps toward providing greater educational opportunities for those who want to be visual artists. In 2008, it established the School of the Arts, a six-year school that also includes academic courses. It is open to Singaporeans and to foreign students. The oldest art school

A celebration marks the beginning of the Singapore Biennale, which is held every two years to showcase new art from around the world.

National Gallery Singapore

National Gallery Singapore opened in 2015 in two historic buildings—Singapore's former Supreme Court and former City Hall. Aluminum tiles have been used to create a modern courtyard that connects the two buildings (left). The National Gallery is the largest art museum in Singapore and the first in the world devoted to Southeast Asian modern art. It displays more than eight thousand pieces of art, from Singapore and all over Southeast Asia.

in Singapore is the Nanyang Academy of Fine Arts (NAFA), which began operating in 1938 and serves more than two thousand students in a typical year. It has excellent courses in the visual arts, and also teaches dance, theater, fashion, and music. NAFA was instrumental in the development of a school of painting known as the Nanyang style in the 1950s. Works in the Nanyang style usually feature outdoor imagery—fishing villages and other shoreline scenes are common—painted with bold lines in vivid watercolors.

The Singapore School of the Arts is Singapore's first high school that focuses on training students in the arts.

Literature

The literature of Singapore has grown tremendously since the nation gained its independence in 1965. Prior to that time, published material from Singaporean authors, regardless of content or style, was scarce at best. Since then, however, many writers have emerged. Although the government keeps an eye on what is published, those wishing to express their views have always found a way to do so.

Many Singaporeans share their thoughts through poetry. Meditation on life in Singapore and what it means to be Singaporean are popular topics. Political subjects—basically forbidden in other artistic forms—have also been successfully explored through poetry. Today's younger poets seem more willing to question the wisdom of the nation's leadership than in past generations. They also delve into questions of religion

A mother reads to her children at the National Library, the nation's largest public library.

Catherine Lim is both a fiction writer and a political commentator.

and the rigid structure of society. Boey Kim Cheng is one of the most respected Singaporean poets. Many of his works deal with memory and the feeling of being separate from the past.

Fiction writing has blossomed among Singaporean writers since the late 1960s. At first, most fiction writers in Singapore focused on short stories. By the 1970s, however, novels by Singaporean authors began gaining attention. Catherine Lim is one of Singapore's most popular authors. Her works often delve into the place of women in Singaporean society. Her books include the short story collection *Little Ironies: Stories of Singapore* (1978) and the novel *Following the Wrong God Home* (2001).

Some modern Singaporean authors write in English and then translate the work themselves into Mandarin Chinese, Malay, or Tamil. Although this can take a tremendous amount of work, it is an opportunity to reach as broad an audience as possible.

Boys look at books during the Singapore Book Fair in 2015. The fair, which features books by more than 150 different publishers, is aimed at getting young people to read.

Music

Singapore is host to a broad array of musical styles. From the time the nation gained its independence, there has been a vibrant musical scene. Even in those early days, when local musicians were influenced by the popular sounds of the Beatles and the Rolling Stones, Singapore was turning out its own hit-makers such as the Crescendos and the October Cherries. Singaporean acts were most likely to find success in Asia and Europe. Today, the Singaporean rock and pop scene is lively, producing internationally known stars such as Stefanie Sun, Tanya Chua, and Mavis Hee.

Stefanie Sun is one of the most popular Singaporean performers. Most of her songs are in Mandarin Chinese, but some are in English.

The Singapore Symphony Orchestra gives a performance in New York.

Singapore also has a strong history of traditional music. Chinese opera houses and music clubs were already a fixture of the city's Chinese neighborhoods a century ago. Chinese opera uses dance, acrobatics, and elaborate makeup and costumes to tell traditional stories. Traditional Malay music, which incorporates drums such as the *kompang* and *hadrah*, is often played at weddings. Likewise, traditional Indian music is performed at many events.

Western classical music is popular in Singapore. The nation's leading orchestra, the Singapore Symphony Orchestra, was founded in 1979. The orchestra has performed to great acclaim around the world. Prominent Singaporean musicians include violinist Lynnette Seah and pianist Abigail Sin.

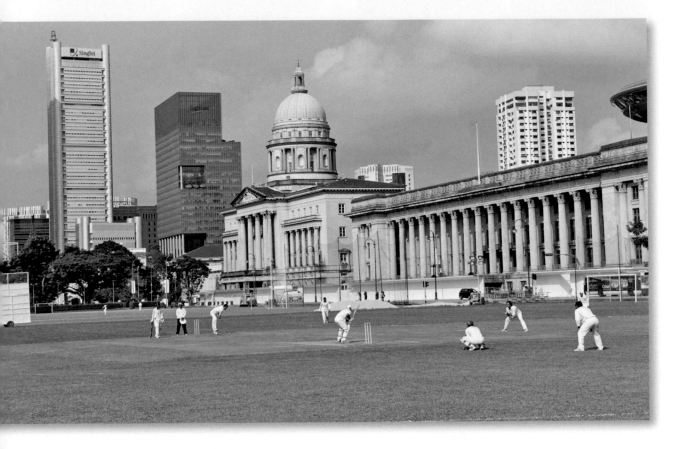

People play cricket in a park near the Singapore City Hall. Cricket is a traditional British sport that is popular in former British colonies around the world.

Sports

The most popular sport in Singapore—and around the world—is soccer. In Singapore, this sport is called football. Singapore also has organized leagues for basketball, cricket, table tennis, bowling, track and field, badminton, and many other sports. The government actively encourages its citizens to stay healthy, so people need not travel far to find a recreation center where they can take part in sports. Since Singapore is an island nation, many people also enjoy water sports. They go swimming, sailing, and snorkeling.

Every four years, athletes from Singapore compete in the Summer Olympics. Singapore usually sends the largest number of athletes to take part in sports such as table tennis, swimming, badminton, and sailing. Although no Singaporean athlete has ever won an Olympic gold medal, they have taken home two silver and two bronze medals. Tan Howe Liang won a silver medal in weight lifting in 1960. The other three medals are more recent. The women's table tennis team won a silver medal in 2008 and a bronze in 2012. And Feng Tianwei, a member of that team, took home a bronze in women's singles in 2012.

Feng Tianwei is one of the top table tennis players in the world.

CHAPTER 10

Day to Day

THE PEOPLE OF SINGAPORE LIVE IN AN EXTREMELY clean and comfortable country with little crime or corruption. There are plenty of jobs, a high standard of living, and an emphasis on getting along with one another. In Singapore, the government encourages people to do their very best in everything—at school, at home, and at work. This emphasis has created an intense drive to succeed among many Singaporeans. They are taught from a young age to focus on their goals.

Government Control

In Singapore, the streets are clean, and visitors will never step on gum that someone has spit out. There's a simple reason for this—gum is not allowed to be imported into the country. In this way and many others, the government plays a large role in the lives of the people of Singapore.

Opposite: **Singaporean Indian girls. The families of many Singaporean Indians have been living in Singapore for five generations or more.**

Singapore schoolchildren on a field trip. In Singapore, the school year is broken up into four terms, with month-long vacations in June and December.

Structure seems to be the norm among Singaporeans, and they accept it. Schoolchildren are well educated and spend long hours in class, receive heavy homework loads, and study extra on weekends and, often, during summer breaks.

While there is little doubt that the government works hard to make sure the people are well taken care of, it comes at the cost of certain personal freedoms. The Singaporean leadership has enacted a number of laws that grant them the power to limit civil liberties. For example, freedom of speech is limited. People cannot speak out against a political party they do not agree with. Anyone who tried would likely get arrested. The government also reserves the right to outlaw any type of content that it considers offensive, even in works of art. Freedom of the press is also limited. Laws determine what can be spread to the public through newspapers, television, radio, and the Internet.

Morning to Night

Most Singaporeans get up early to start the day. It is not unusual for both adults and children to get up around 6:30 a.m. They take a quick shower, dress, eat breakfast, gather their things, and head out the door. For adults, this means fighting the sometimes brutal traffic to reach their jobs by 8:00 or 9:00 a.m. For schoolchildren, classes often start as early as 7:30 a.m.

The midday break comes around noon. Some children eat lunch they brought from home or purchase lunch in the cafeteria. The length of lunch and recess vary with the school, but it usually lasts about a half hour and then the children head back to class. The school day ends around 2:30 or 3:00 p.m.

Children relax in the cafeteria in a school in Singapore.

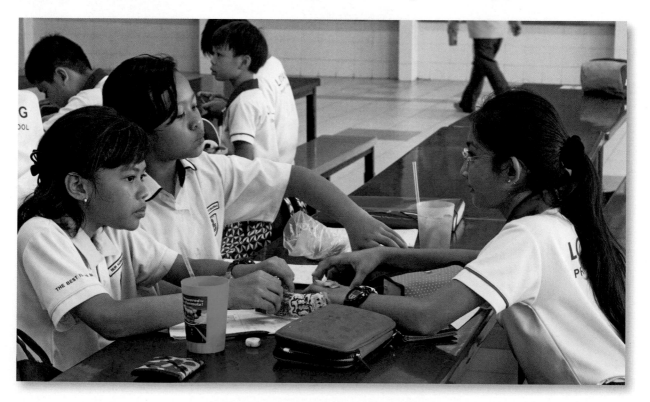

After school, many children go right into an extracurricular activity. Sports are common, with many children playing soccer, badminton, or table tennis.

Children get home in the late afternoon and dive right into their homework. Dinner is served around 6:30 or 7:00 p.m. It is an important time for the family, when everyone shares their thoughts and experiences from the day. After dinner, everyone can relax. Families might watch TV, play a game, or walk the dog. People begin to get ready for bed around 9:00 p.m., and everyone is asleep no later than 10:00 p.m.

Children play many different sports in Singapore, including rugby.

Getting Around

Although Singapore is a large, bustling city, getting around is generally quite simple. The public transportation system is known for being clean, efficient, and affordable. Singapore has both a rail system and buses. In most areas, public transportation runs from around 5:30 a.m. until midnight and costs just a dollar or two per trip. Taxis are also widely available. They can be hailed during hours when buses and trains aren't running. They are, however, more expensive than buses and trains.

Since Singapore is an island nation of relatively small size, the government prefers as few private cars on the road as possible. Although people have the option of owning a car, the government discourages it. The permits needed to buy a car cost tens of thousands of dollars. Singaporeans also have the option of owning a motorcycle, but that too is generally discouraged.

Many children in Singapore take public transportation to school.

Bikes parked at a commuter train station. Owning a car is very expensive in Singapore, so most people bike or take public transportation to work.

For Singaporeans who live relatively close to their jobs, bicycles have become a popular choice. They are affordable, do not pollute the environment, and offer the extra benefit of promoting the health of the rider.

Home and Family

The people of Singapore place great emphasis on fostering strong family relationships in the home. Most households in Singapore consist of two parents and one or more children. About 85

National Holidays

New Year's Day	January 1
Chinese New Year	February
Good Friday	March or April
Labour Day	May 1
Vesak (Buddha's birthday)	April or May
National Day	August 9
Deepavali	October or November
Christmas	December 25

Two Muslim holidays are also celebrated as national holidays: Hari Raya Puasa and Hari Raya Haji. Because the Islamic calendar is eleven days shorter than the Western calendar, these holidays fall on different days from year to year.

percent of all Singapore families fall into this category. Adult children often stay at home until they are ready to marry.

Children are taught from an early age to behave themselves and to be considerate to others. In particular, they are expected to show their elders a great deal of respect. In the typical household, the eldest members have the greatest social standing. Children understand that they will eventually be responsible for the care of their elderly relatives.

Cuisine

The food of Singapore is as diverse as the nation itself, featuring dishes that have their roots in the cultures of neighboring countries such China, India, and Indonesia, as well as in European countries that have played a role in Singaporean history, such as England and Holland.

Kaya Toast

Kaya toast makes a delicious breakfast. It is also frequently eaten in the afternoon, with a cup of tea. Have an adult help you with this recipe.

Ingredients

1 cup coconut milk
2 slices white bread
1 cup sugar
1 tablespoon shaved salted butter
$1/8$ teaspoon salt
1 teaspoon soy sauce
4 eggs
Dash ground white pepper
3 egg yolks
1 soft-boiled egg, peeled

Directions

To make the coconut jam, mix together the coconut milk, ½ cup sugar, and the salt in a small pot. Place the pot on the stove and bring the mixture to a boil over high heat. In a stainless steel mixing bowl, whisk together 3 eggs, 3 yolks, and the other ½ cup sugar. Stir in the coconut milk mixture to make the custard. Place the stainless steel bowl over a medium pot of lightly simmering water. Gently cook the custard, stirring constantly, until the custard thickens, about 15 to 20 minutes. This will produce about 2 cups of coconut jam, enough for many sandwiches.

Toast two slices of bread. Spread coconut jam on both slices of bread and put the shaved butter on top of the jam. Put the two pieces of bread together to form a sandwich. Cut the sandwich in half.

On the stovetop, slowly fry an egg in a nonstick pan. When the white of the egg has set, remove it and place in on a plate next to the sandwich. Pour the soy sauce over the egg and add a dash of pepper. Enjoy!

In Singapore, breakfast can be practically anything. Kaya toast—toast with coconut jam and an egg—is popular. Many people enjoy noodles for breakfast. *Chwee kueh*—steamed rice cakes with preserved radish—is common. Dumplings are also a good option. Coffee is a popular drink at breakfast, as is tea.

Throughout the day, seafood is a popular choice for meals. People eat shrimp, prawns, crab, fish, and much more. These foods are cooked in dozens of different ways, served with rice or noodles or in soup. Fish are often made into cakes, pastes, or dried and eaten as snacks.

Soups are particularly beloved in Singapore. One popular soup is *bak kut teh*, a dish that originated in China and features pork ribs in a soup filled with fragrant spices such as cloves, cinnamon, fennel, and anise. Chicken, beef, duck, and tofu are often used in soups as well as other dishes.

The people of Singapore enjoy many different kinds of fruit. One of the most popular is durian, a large fruit covered in thorns that is famous for its very strong odor. The odor is so unpleasant, in fact, that people are not allowed to take durians on the trains and buses in Singapore. There are "No Durian" signs on train platforms right next to the "No Smoking" signs. Singaporeans enjoy durians fresh, or use them as an ingredient in custards, cakes, and many other foods. Other popular fruits in Singapore include lychees, longans, coconuts, and mangosteens.

When they get hungry, many Singaporeans head to hawker centers. These are huge markets filled with stalls, each one selling a different kind of food. The food is cheap, wide-ranging, and delicious. One person can get Hainanese chicken and rice, a dish popular in China. Another can get a Malay dish called *laksa* that features noodles with fish cakes and prawns slathered in a thick, creamy coconut sauce. A third person can get *roti prata*, a fried pancake of Indian origin sprinkled with curry.

Durian fruit is covered with sharp spikes that are difficult to cut through.

Singaporeans take great pride in their cuisine. They consider good food a part of the national identity and they love sitting down to a great meal. Although many Singaporean dishes originated elsewhere, the people of Singapore have altered the dishes to make them uniquely their own, and they cook them with passion.

Most Singaporeans eat out frequently. They often go to hawker centers, where they have a huge variety of food choices.

Timeline

SINGAPOREAN HISTORY		WORLD HISTORY	
		ca. 2500 BCE	The Egyptians build the pyramids and the Sphinx in Giza.
		ca. 563 BCE	The Buddha is born in India.
The first written record of humans in Singapore is created.	**100s CE**	**313 CE**	The Roman emperor Constantine legalizes Christianity.
		610	The Prophet Muhammad begins preaching a new religion called Islam.
The Chola kingdom of India invades the island.	**1025**	**1054**	The Eastern (Orthodox) and Western (Roman Catholic) Churches break apart.
Srivijaya prince Sri Tri Buana lands in Singapore.	**1200s**	**1095**	The Crusades begin.
		1215	King John seals the Magna Carta.
Warring factions vie for control of Singapore.	**1300s**	**1300s**	The Renaissance begins in Italy.
		1347	The plague sweeps through Europe.
The Sultanate of Malacca gains control of Singapore.	**1400s**	**1453**	Ottoman Turks capture Constantinople, conquering the Byzantine Empire.
		1492	Columbus arrives in North America.
Portugal becomes dominant in the region.	**Early 1500s**	**1500s**	Reformers break away from the Catholic Church, and Protestantism is born.
		1776	The U.S. Declaration of Independence is signed.
		1789	The French Revolution begins.
Sir Thomas Raffles opens a British trading post in Singapore.	**1819**		
Singapore joins the Straits Settlements.	**1826**	**1865**	The American Civil War ends.
		1879	The first practical lightbulb is invented.

SINGAPOREAN HISTORY		WORLD HISTORY	
		World War I begins.	1914
		The Bolshevik Revolution brings communism to Russia.	1917
		A worldwide economic depression begins.	1929
		World War II begins.	1939
Japanese troops invade Singapore.	1941		
Japan surrenders at the end of World War II; Singapore reverts to British control.	1945	World War II ends.	1945
Singapore becomes self-governing.	1959		
Singapore joins the federation of Malaysia.	1963		
Singapore leaves the federation of Malaysia and becomes fully independent.	1965		
		Humans land on the Moon.	1969
Great Britain ends its military defense of Singapore.	1971		
		The Vietnam War ends.	1975
		The Berlin Wall is torn down as communism crumbles in Eastern Europe.	1989
		The Soviet Union breaks into separate states.	1991
		Terrorists attack the World Trade Center in New York City and the Pentagon near Washington, D.C.	2001
Singapore and the United States sign a free trade agreement.	2003	A tsunami in the Indian Ocean destroys coastlines in Africa, India, and Southeast Asia.	2004
Singapore's economy suffers during a worldwide economic downturn.	2008	The United States elects its first African American president.	2008
Singapore legalizes casino gambling.	2010		

Fast Facts

Official name: The Republic of Singapore

Capital: Singapore

Year of founding: 1959

City Hall

National flag

Sungei Buloh Wetland Reserve

Official languages: English, Mandarin Chinese, Malay, Tamil

Official religion: None

National anthem: "Majulah Singapura" ("Onward Singapore")

Type of government: Republic

Head of government: Prime Minister

Head of state: President

Neighboring countries: Malaysia is the nearest country, lying across the Strait of Johor

Area: 278 square miles (720 sq km)

Latitude and longitude: 1.3° N, 103.8° E

Northernmost point: Coast of Sembawang, around the Senoko Industrial Estate

Southernmost point: Satumu Island

Westernmost point: Tuas Island

Easternmost point: Pedra Branca Island

Highest elevation: Timah Hill, 531 feet (162 m) above sea level

Lowest elevation: Sea level along the coasts

Hottest month: June, with an average temperature of about 82°F (28°C)

Coolest month: January, with an average temperature of about 79°F (26°C)

Average annual precipitation: 92 inches (234 cm)

Skyscrapers

Currency

National population (2014 est.): 5,487,000

Landmarks:
- ▶ *Baba House*
- ▶ *Bukit Timah Nature Reserve*
- ▶ *National Gallery Singapore*
- ▶ *Singapore Botanic Gardens*
- ▶ *Singapore Zoo*

Economy: Singapore has a robust economy. It is a center of banking and trade, and tourism has become important. Singapore is also one of the world's leading locations for oil refining. Electronics, chemicals, medicines, and transportation equipment are all manufactured in Singapore. The nation has little room for agriculture, but it is one of the world's leading producers of orchids. Chickens, cabbage, spinach, and lettuce are also grown there.

Currency: The Singapore dollar. In 2015, S$1 equaled US$0.71, and US$1.00 equaled S$1.40.

System of weights and measures: Metric system

Literacy rate : 96%

Schoolchildren

Feng Tianwei

Common Malay words and phrases:

Ya	Yes
Tidak	No
Selamat pagi	Good morning
Selamat tinggal	Good-bye (said if you're leaving)
Selamat jalan	Good-bye (said if you're staying)
Semoga hari anda baik sahaja.	Have a nice day.
Berapa harganya ini?	How much is this?
Terima kasih	Thank you

Prominent Singaporeans:

Boey Kim Cheng   (1965–)
Poet

Feng Tianwei   (1986–)
Table tennis champion

Yusof bin Ishak   (1910–1970)
President

Lee Kuan Yew   (1923–2015)
President

Catherine Lim   (1942–)
Author

Thomas Raffles   (1781–1826)
Founder of Singapore

Stefanie Sun   (1978–)
Singer and songwriter

To Find Out More

Books

▶ Layton, Leslie, and Guek-Cheng Pan. *Singapore*. New York: Cavendish Square, 2012.

▶ Owings, Lisa. *Singapore*. Minneapolis: Bellwether Media, 2014.

▶ Phillips, Douglas A. *Southeast Asia*. New York: Chelsea House, 2009.

Music

▶ Chua, Tanya. *Stranger*. New York: Warner Music, 2003.

▶ Singapore Symphony Orchestra. *Debussy: La Mer*. Akersberga, Sweden, 2014.

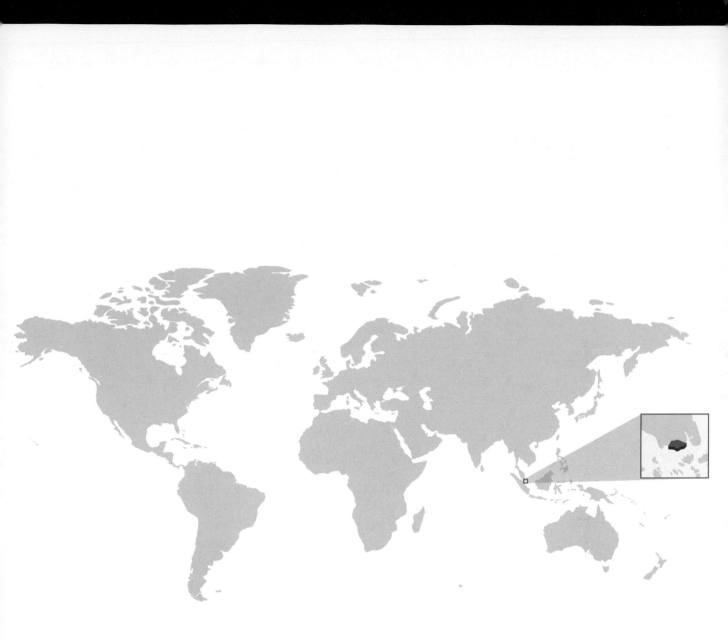

▶ Visit this Scholastic Web site for more information on Singapore:
www.factsfornow.scholastic.com
Enter the keyword **Singapore**

Index

Page numbers in *italics* indicate illustrations.

Thomas Raffles, 45–46, 47, *47*
trade and, 29, 43–46, *45*
World War II and, 50, *50*, 51, 53
gum, 117
Guthrie company, 48

H

hawker centers, 125, *127*
health care, 89, *89*
Hee, Mavis, 112
herons, 36
High Court, 62, *63*
Hinduism. *See also* religion.
followers of, 95, 100, *101*
Indian people and, 100
philosophy of, 100–101
Sri Mariamman Temple, *100*
Srivijaya empire, 100
historical maps. *See also* maps.
British Trade Routes, 19th
Century, *45*
Early Kingdoms, *42*
holidays
national, *58*, 123
religious, 102
housing, 38, 54, *72*, *91*

I

imports
coal, 27
food, 69
foreign trade, 54, 78
gum, 117
natural gas, 27, 69
oil, 27, 69
taxes on, 54
transportation of, *78*
water, 25, 69
independence. *See also* government.
constitution and, 57
elections and, *52*, 53
Great Britain and, 54

national anthem and, 67
National Day, 58
national flag and, 62
World War II and, 53
Indian people. *See also* people.
children, *116*
early trade and, 41
ethnic groups, 82, 87
Islamic religion and, 98
music, 113
population of, 10, 81
Tamil language, 87
Indonesia
foods and, 123
islands, 17, 41
Java, 42, *43*
languages in, 86
Majapahit Palace, *43*
Sumatra, 41
trade with, 78
infant mortality rate, 89
infrastructure, 54
insect life, 31, 36
Internet, 118
irrigation, 26
Ishak, Yusof bin, 79, 133
Islamic religion. *See also* religion.
Ahmadi Muslims, 98
education and, *13*
followers of, *82*, 95, 98
Indian people and, 98
Muhammad (prophet), 98
prayer, 98
Qur'an (holy book), 98
Shia Muslims, 98
Sultan Mosque, 98
Sunni Muslims, 98

J

Japan, 50–53
Javanese language, 42, 82
Jehovah's Witnesses, 102–103

Jesus Christ, 97
Joaquim, Agnes, 34
Johor Strait, 17
judicial branch of government, 59,
61–62, *63*
Jurong Island, 19, *19*, 24

K

kaya toast, 124, *124*, 125
king cobras, 38–39
Kranji War Cemetery, 53
Kranji War Memorial, 53, *53*

L

languages. *See* Chinese languages;
English language; Javanese
language; Malay language; Tamil
language.
Laozi (philosopher), 99, *99*
Lee Hsien Loong, *60*
Lee Kuan Yew, 11, 61, 133
legislative branch of government, 59,
60–61
Lim, Catherine, 110, *110*, 133
literature
Boey Kim Cheng, 110, 133
Catherine Lim, 110, *110*, 133
Chinese language and, 111
English language and, 111
fiction, 110
government and, 109
Malay language and, 111
poetry, 109–110, 133
Tamil language and, 111
livestock, 76
long-tailed parakeets, 37

M

Mahayana Buddhism, 96
Majapahit kingdom, 42
Majapahit Palace (Indonesia), *43*

Meet the Author

WIL MARA IS THE AWARD-WINNING author of more then 140 books, many of them educational titles for children in Scholastic's catalog. He began writing in the late 1980s with several nonfiction titles about herpetology. He branched out into fiction in the mid-1990s, when he ghostwrote five of the popular Boxcar Children Mysteries. He has since authored more than a dozen novels, including *Wave*, which was a recipient of the 2005 New Jersey Notable Book Award, *The Gemini Virus*, and the *New York Times* best seller *Frame 232*, which reached the number one spot in its category on Amazon .com and won the 2013 Lime Award for Excellence in Fiction.

Photo Credits